POETIC PEACE

The Heart-felt Edition

Lawrence Irchirl Jr

Poetic Peace: The Heart-felt Edition
Copyright © 2025 by Lawrence Irchirl Jr.

All rights reserved. No part of this publication may be reproduced, distributed, or transmitted in any form or by any means, including photocopying, recording, or other electronic or mechanical methods, without the written consent of the publisher. The only exceptions are for brief quotations included in critical reviews and other noncommercial uses permitted by copyright law.

MILTON & HUGO L.L.C.
1001 3rd Avenue West, Suite 430
Bradenton, FL 34205, USA

Website: *www. miltonandhugo.com*
Hotline: *1- 888-778-0033*
Email: *info@miltonandhugo.com*

Ordering Information:
Quantity sales. Special discounts are granted to corporations, associations, and other organizations. For more information on these discounts, please reach out to the publisher using the contact information provided above.

ISBN-13:	979-8-89285-766-6	[Paperback Edition]
	979-8-89285-767-3	[Hardback Edition]
	979-8-89285-765-9	[Digital Edition]

Rev. date: 12/17/2025

Introduction

If you've picked up this book, I pray that everything inside of it heals you. I hope that every moment I spent wondering if I would ever get my message to the ears that needed the nourishment beat a sound of love so beautiful into your soul that just as I healed, may you do the same. I know that we don't all have the same beliefs and perspectives, I think it's quite fascinating how many opinions can be had about one topic, but in this book I don't aim to offend anyone. I aim to express the gift I never knew I had, and I heard it helps people. I'll be speaking with voice like this throughout the whole book. I want you to feel the human voice as you read through my life. From high school when I was a kid preparing to take on the world, to post-graduation looking for my way in the world. If you pick up this book, may you purchase the healing journey that you needed. And one more thing before we get started, I want to say thank you to both my parents for creating a creator. Now let's go to freshman year of high school, where my writing journey and your healing process would only begin.

High School

High School

You sellin' lies and I was the monopsony,
Then you killed my heart, no need for the autopsy.
Did you plan to do it? Premeditated murder?
Let's discuss this and go a little further.
So now with cold blood coursin' through my veins
I'm part of the walkin' dead, am I insane?
Nah I was just drunk in love or was it love on the brain,   (1.5x)
Man, what's the difference, it all seem the same.
Do you finally see what your lies have done to me?   (1.5x)
Do you see how hate for you should be overcoming me?
No?, stop! Come back, don't run from me!   (2x)
Truth hurt don't it? Like when I found out you had no love for me. (2x-1.5x)
Yeah…so should I avenge myself for the way I feel?   (1.5x-1.0)
Nah cause I've allowed the pain to be reveal, but it hurt still.
So I inhale, exhale, prevail, so to YOU, YOUR LIES, & MY PAIN,…I say farewell.

Poet's words: So where you see the (2x) and the (1.5x) these are reading speeds and if you're going to read the poems and understand why they are written that way, pace will be important. So let me explain, the 2x means to read at double the speed while the 1.5 means to read at half a speed faster than you would normally. If it is in all caps I am definitely emphasizing those phrases. I didn't write "and", I chose to use the "&" instead because I don't emphasize "and" when writing it. Last but not least, a comma (,) means to pause, which is what gives it the rhythm that you're wanting. However, if you see "..." after a comma, that means take a long pause, take a deep breath. I think that's all. We're warmed up now though on to the next one.

Girl Problems

Girl problem number what? Man…I forgot,
But it land in a spot.
It got a girl I don't even know,
but she a friend of my bro.
I watched from a distance to find her personality,
and she seems a lot like me.
She what I'd consider fine,
I would love it if she was mine.
I can't help but see, she be kind of watchin' me
but in a shy type of way,
I wonder if its cause she don't know what to say.
Anyway, just put this near girl problem number 3,
and just leave the solving to me.

Poet's Words: Ok, so nobody said you had to be great to start, but…you do have to start to be great. So, this obviously is my 3rd piece written, don't hate me too much for it. It does get significantly better. Just wait till you hear my senior year and how we go out with a pen on fire. Just jokes, lighten up! No, you may not be exactly where you want to be but if you're going to be more than you currently are you have to start taking small steps. Get started.

Hopeless Love

Don't wanna go outside and play,
I would rather stay in the house today.
I gotta go to the gym tonight,
but first I want to write,
about a girl I've seen for a while
I must admit I was excited when she gave me her number to dial,
I didn't think the number was real,
and I almost passed on a once in a lifetime deal.
If this was a dream I didn't want to wake up,
but it was real and it made me perk up.
When I realized the number wasn't a fake,
I stopped what I was doin' to take a break,
and text her to see how she was doin'
cause I didn't want to ruin,
my chances if I could ever have any to call her mine,
many many times but I'll stop my rhymes,
if she says she'll be mine.

Poet's Words: Spoiler Alert: She did not in fact say she would be mine. Thus you got this book, because I continued my rhymes. All in good humor, I say that to say that while the rhythm is choppy and the rhyme scheme was quite basic, the process is the most important part to progress. You never know which doors get slammed in your face so that you have the chance to walk through better doors. If I had stopped writing due to any of my heart breaks, I would've never discovered who I am. Being alone isn't the worse thing in the world, because that's where you experience the difference between solitude and loneliness. But there's nothing wrong with getting butterflies and wanting to write about it, as I did.

The Encounter

Every girl watches her physique,
whether they watch it grow or watch it shrink
some are obsessed while others are blessed.
Speakin of which reminds me of a girl I once knew,
and unlike most her figure was true.
I didn't know her name but I was eager to find out
or maybe just to know what she was about,
and I figured I'd never have a chance,
but that all changed in one glance,
one day in the hall when I passed her by,
and somehow I was able to catch her eye.
And I know that we felt the same way,
the only downer was I didn't know what to say,
it was a moment for which I was unprepared
and I let get away because I was scared,
of what, something that had no chance of happening,
I couldn't even talk to a girl I was attracting,
she was the only thing I could think about for the next few days,
so now I feel like a player who needs knew plays,
and by the grace of God I get a second chance
so now my life has changed in one glance
only this time she's with her friends
but I can't let that matter cause in 5 minutes my opportunity ends.

So I swallow my fear and start to walk her way
but in my mind I have not a clue what I am to say,
she stares at me the whole mile,
but the way she did it was with a welcoming smile
so I start the encounter with just a simple "hi"
but I was nervous so I did sound shy,
she answered back with a calm "hey"
to send me spiraling for something else to say
so I told her my name
and she followed by doing the same,
now comes the part that requires pride
so for me I had to reach deep down inside
to ask her if I could have her number,
just to talk to her before she began to slumber,
she must have laughed for at least 3 minutes
so I figured now is when it's time to pack my bags and walk away
but as I began she told me to stay
and asked me for pencil and paper
then she said to call her later.
So now I walk to class with not only a girl's number
but a girl to dream about when I slumber.

Poet's Words: Sounds like I'm starting to learn concepts, hold your lunch, it might get a little weird for a second. Think of it kind of like a metamorphosis, it's beautiful in the end but it can be dark in the process. Can I get an E for effort though? Ok, moving on. Well I guess first you deserve to know what this one has to do with your healing process. You will experiment with things you like and you have a natural gravitation toward and it may look awkward at first but don't let the outside world stop you from doing what you like and you're good at. It may even feel unnatural at first but life is not to be lived completely in comfort. Go explore!

Misunderstood Passion

Blood bursting with anger and aggression,
I'm not catholic but Father please allow me this confession.
I know you must look down and wonder why I allow these things to trouble me, especially after giving me this talent poetically.
It's just…I don't destroy dreams but when I have 'em, I seem to be stuck tryna make 'em disappear like magic.
I have to hide my ideas because they'll never be good enough,
and Father you know how he crushes them with the slightest touch.
You know how I look up to him feelin' like I'll never measure up,
so I always pray to you to help me up.
I know hate is wrong but I think I'm losing love,
so if you're too busy please send me an angel from above.
Father I'm breakin' but tryna keep the faith,
I just need a few moments to feel as though I'm safe.
Please come quick to one of your children
and bring with you, the power of your healing.

Poet's Words: Believe it or not, I'm not just a page with words, I am the voice of a person, who has real emotions just like you. That means that people aim to discourage me from doing things they don't think that they can accomplish, that means that every idea is not always met with constructive criticism, that means that, I too feel alone when surrounded by the ones I'm closest to. That does not mean that I love them less or that I grow hatred toward them for comments they made that affected me in ways they were unaware of. That's what this piece is, it's hurt from the perspective of betrayal and I feel the only one I can turn to is God. That's just what I believe in, and you'll see later how it helps but I won't spoil the ending for you.

Careful Cases

Bleeding internally,...
I been shot! Could somebody be planning to murder me? (2x-1.5x)
What did I do wrong?! I mean have they hear of me?   (1.5x)
Rushing me to the hospital hopin to save my life with surgery, (1.5x)
I'm just hopin to make it out like a baby in the nursery.
Surgeons cut me open only to see my life is hopeless cause when they looked inside something different is what they noticed.
A heart that had just been shattered on impact, taking pain that could never be taken back.
And that day was the last time I was seen,
so be careful what you say...cause some things you don't mean.

Poet's Words: So obviously, I got my feelings hurt. Want some ironic humor? I don't even remember WHO I wrote this about. However, I appreciate younger me learning to develop use of concepts and developing imagery. Things that evoke the emotions the same strength that I felt. Did I think this was great when I wrote it? Honestly, I thought it was the greatest thing I'd ever write, but thank God it gets better or this book wouldn't even exist. As we turn the page, just remember that you too have a gift, even if you haven't discovered what it is yet. Lord knows I didn't know I would even keep writing.

Mercedes

Smile simple but deep enough to touch my heart.
I can feel the pain, stress and insecurities tearing her apart. (1.5x)
I can see the things missed in her childhood, (1.5x)
but that's real, so you can't rewind like Hollywood.
And just when life was tryna drive her crazy,
I opened her mind to new thoughts and her name was Mercedes.
She seemed so familiar but so foreign
so now she racing through my head like there was no time for touring. (1.5x)
She got me daydreaming about a test drive, but wait... (1.5x)
slam the brakes, am I the next guy?
This movin kinda fast like NASCAR (2x)
and I hate squares but she seem well rounded so far. (2x)
Hasn't been a week but I think I'd bankrupt for the body like a benz (1.5x)
so now I'm daydreaming and the fantasies begin.
I can see the smirk on her face that makes me want to taste her lips
as she's completely clueless the charm that she drips.
Her braces make it harder to make me not do the unexpected,

cause I feel if I did then she'd just reflect it.
And now I hope she turns blush like the rose that she is
cause when it comes to smelling good she seems to be the wiz'.
I hope this makes her night and I make her dreams
cause I've been trying since day one, so it seems.
So now she knows somewhat how I feel
but I speak in illusions so she'll have to use her head lights to know what's real. But much love to the one who knows what I'm talking about
cause you felt the same with no doubt.

Poet's Words: The first time I ACTUALLY wrote for a young lady because she asked me to. If I only knew now what I knew then...but that's what life is for. It's a learning process and we should be learning everyday. Enjoy the moments, those are the fabric of your life so make sure to create a bunch of them. When you're too old to be young, you'll only have a memory of your younger self so be expressive, take a risk or two so that you have stories to tell...or not tell. Either way, live in the moment, plan for the future, and it'll make looking back at the past a lot more fun. This piece is like a time capsule, I can always look back and think of how young and dumb I was but I can also see my growth. This was a part of my high school memories. Long story short, life is to be experienced. A beautiful piece (for high school me) for a beautiful young lady. Now let's keep moving.

Poetic Painting

They say a picture's worth a thousand words,
so if my words paint a picture, what's that worth?
And if my words paint a picture of who I am,
does that mean I could have a value determined by currency
or would my value still be unknown…like currently?
What if I don't want a net worth cause I'm scared of getting caught up in it all,
and then I think, do my thoughts matter at all.
Or are they just another perspective soon to be dismissed,
as people would throw them away to never again reminisce.
But my words will continue to draw on this canvas as they try to erase
but I won't speed up or slow down, I'll maintain my pace.
I won't let the things around me control how I behave
and I'll speak my freedom until I rest in my grave.
But my number one goal is that I live on when I rest easy,
and I hope somebody finishes my movement cause that'll complete me.
That's the true meaning behind my name
because without meaning nothing else will remain.

Signed Poetic Peace coming back as soon as possible, but in the meantime help the movement to become unstoppable.

Poet's Words: So…, in high school the name I wanted to be known by during open mics and any other performances, was Poetic Peace because my writing was therapeutic but I was also somewhat ashamed of sharing it, because having a soft side and expressing your emotions wasn't always the "cool" thing to do in high school. However, I noticed the more people heard what I wrote, the more they would pull me to the side and tell me how they appreciated me sharing because they too felt the same. Why is this relevant? That thing that you're really good at but you're hiding from the world is the same thing the world would love you for sharing. The ironic part about this lifetime is that whatever you are scared of, somebody else is too, but together we have nothing to fear. And that was my vision in high school, a world where everybody expresses themselves in a creative way to make the world a more connected and beautifully healed place. So,…if something happens to me and you're reading this, you've officially signed up to continue the mission if it takes longer than my lifetime. Just JOKING,…kind of. But we're almost through high school so let's keep going.

My Last Ride

Grew up together so it's only understandable we grew apart (1.5x)
but no love loss so please don't take it to heart,
but wait that's senior year so let me start from the beginning
cause I remember class of '13 was screamin' "yeah we winnin".
But that was 8th grade when we ran it like a boss,
but now we freshmen so the title has been lost.
And we was too excited to see we was below the totem poles,
but at least keepin our unity didn't need to be a goal.
Then bonds were made some deeper than others, (1.5x)
went from callin each other bros to callin each other brothers.
Now the clock has started movin and it's sophomore year,
and some of life's lessons start to draw near.
Remember that same girl who was quiet and seem to keep her head down,
well it just so happen she did one thing and her name got around.
Her story got overexaggerated and now she got a petty name,
but I know her story so to me she still the same.

Now I see the Great Divide happening as history is in it's repetition,
so now I think when my parents speak, I should probably pay attention.
People I've known for years look me in my eyes and don't speak,
and those were the same people askin me for something the following week.
But I always remember you gotta love those who overlook you,
but for me I always said that was a part of me being Pooh.
Pooh was how I defined myself sophomore year,
cause that's who I'd always been even before I made a year.
I didn't mind changing I just didn't wanna lose myself,
so in my mind that defining moment is on top of my greatness shelf.
And I know some will laugh and say my name is funny,
but my names mean more to me than any amount of money.
I truly understand human creativity,
so now when I hear names I contemplate as they interest me.
They're graffiti from others painted into the air of how they see you,
whether they love you, hate you, or just wanna be you.
I'm not Derrick but if you call a rose by another name,
I know for sure the smell remains the same.

So I guess you could say Shakespeare taught me to worry about my fragrance
and that I can only strengthen it with my patience.
That's two years down so no I'm over half way there,
when I met a girl who got me to stop and stare.
She showed me love was blind and she was no braille,
but I tried with her anyway setting myself up to fail.
I fought for what I thought was real for 10 months,
felt like a decade but I never thought to turn back, not once.
She showed me being smart can't stop you from being a fool,
cause "love" does it to us all then we drown ourselves in a pool.
Whether it be a pool of drugs or illusions
it'll chill your heart if you let it sink you into confusion.
That was my junior year
but I found myself never knowing I was lost in fear.
So now I'm back where I started, as a senior
so now you can see the reason for my demeanor.
You've seen how people come and go
and how myself is what I know.
That's what high school is all about,
giving you the chance to know yourself with no doubt.
So I thank you for lending me an ear
cause to come up here my heart was shakin with fear.
Signed and sealed Poetic Peace,
speakin with my voice until I'm decease.
And if I could ask one more favor,

stand up and put your hands together like you was sayin a prayer.
And I'm closing quick but first I gotta thank Ayam Ovel, Money Makin Myles, TJ and all others that influence me,
I'm not KD but y'all the real MVP.

Poet's Words: Welcome to the end of senior year, baby! We made it, WE HERE NOW!! We the ones on the mountain top, WE THE ONES GRADUATING!! Sad part is the people I've known the majority of my life, told my secrets to, had my greatest laughs with, share childhood memories with, I'll never even see again. One day I'll go "that's my classmate" instead of "that's my bro". So, this piece was truly the kiss goodbye to one chapter of life, and a hopeful hello to the next...Even if I did have to highjack the stage TO SAY THIS AT GRADUATION! Go chiefs! (my high school mascot). The lesson here is there will be some things you have to let go to get to be the person you want to be. Enjoy your ignorance while seeking knowledge. Enjoy the moments in life where you're surrounded by great people while doing what you love. This may take trial and error, it may not, but it will take time.

University

The Last Hope

Four seeds planted and so they all grew,
but not to their full potential, especially the first two.
(1x-0.5x)
Now, imagine those seeds are people
taking on life, both the good and evil   (1.5x)
and of the four one of 'em ain't got a fighting chance (1.5x)
but you prolly wouldn't guess that with the way he plays his hand. (1.5x)
He was born with legs that don't always support (1.5x)
but at least he still tryin like granny say "thank the Lort". (1.5x)
But back to the first two seeds,
the first two to carry on the family tree.
Well, the first began to make her own way,
she stop praying stop listening so there was nothing more to say.
Never say her diploma and still don't see how it hurt her today.
So I just shake my head cause again there's nothing more to say.
As for the next seed, she has a better chance she can watch and learn to better her future plans.
Things seem to be going great she finally got her diploma

but after that, sad to say, her success was over.
She got strung out on street pharmacy so having to lose two sisters like that was hard for me.
Now I don't know if you kept count but there's only one seed left
and well I'm that seed and I'm doing my best.
First seed to make it to a college campus
and I wanna release the stress but who really gone understand this?
When the game on the line with the ball in your hands (2x)
and you the underdog so no support from fans. (2x)
When the only ones on your sideline are the ones that had something to do with your creation, (2x)
so tell me how many would really understand if I brought it to conversation. (1.5x)
So, I'm the last hope and when it gets to be too much, writing is how I cope.
My listeners love it for reasons I may never know,
but the question is will I make it, I hope so. (0.5x)

Poet's Words: Welcome to my VERY FIRST poem written in college. This was literally within a week of me stepping foot onto Louisiana Tech University's campus, and I remember writing it for the annual 7:11 show. This was the first piece I ever performed on a stage. This piece was my first encore. In many ways this piece was my first, from the attention and recognition, to learning the elements of performance on a stage. Feeling butterflies in a new place where I don't know anybody. The only thing that would comfort me in this moment was knowing that most people who leave home to go to a university feel this way in one way or another. See, this is why you don't skip the process. The process prepares you in ways you never knew you needed. Let's keep going, it only gets better from here. Warning: the poetry may get darker with life problems but there's no story without conflict.

Mitchell

Spent so many nights between the phone booth and the mirror,
tryna find somebody to talk to as to why I feel inferior.
But I forgot to mention the booths don't have phones and the mirror don't show signs of reassurance,
so now my eyes sweating while my heart practicing endurance.
Cause I keep calling to my Father for help,
but I keep being asked to save someone else.
I keep helping those with my same problems thinkin they could understand my pain,
but my flaw coming in thinking we built the same.
(1x-0.5x
See He cursed me with this S on my chest,
cause He knew before you saw the cross you'd need to be blessed.
So when you look at me you see the moon,
just a window dimming the glow for what'll be back soon.
And that sound real cute but that don't help my mental,
I still need to talk about everything I been through.
Like I need to tell somebody what it's like to not be able to hug my mama when I'm breaking down,

how long I gotta hold back these tears to cry when nobody else is around.
How I laugh to only temporarily numb the pain,
but deep down knowing that everyday I'm goin insane.
I don't even live in the present cause it cut so deep,
instead I reminisce on the past just to go to sleep.
That the only signs I give of my depression
are the black clothes in which I dress in,
but nobody notices that everyday a piece of me dies so now I confess it.
But sometimes I have to question how I can still wear my heart on my sleeve,
I guess some things are eternal like the effect from Adam and Eve.
And now my eyes start burning and heart trembling just to write this far,
and now you probably want to hug me almost congratulating me for making it this far.
But I don't need your hugs, I don't need your sympathy, (1.5x)
I don't need you to feel for me, I don't need empathy. (1.5x)
I don't need...I don't know I just don't need anything you haven't already given,
I don't even need you to listen, I'll just "thug it out" like I always do,
and be wearing all black and a smile the next time I see you.
Cause I just need the love my grandmother left me and the cards life dealt me,
to continue to be the bridge I was meant to be.

And ladies please after hearing this don't let me play
the strings to your heart, giving you thoughts that you
can fix something that's constantly falling apart.
Trust me there is no saving a savior,
it's a lonely existence of misunderstood behavior.
But for this piece I'll probably get encores and tissues,
and how soon you forget all the pain and issues, that I
went through (1.5x-1.0x)
to speak this at a venue.
But I don't need you to be there for me when I'm
feeling inferior, (0.5x)
cause I got these phone booths and this mirror. This is
Mitchell. (0.5x)

Poet's Words: Yeahhh, I warned you on the last poem didn't I? Mitchell was a dorm that was once upon a time on Louisiana Tech's campus and let's just say it wasn't the Ritz Carlton. However, at this point I'm learning college life all while balancing real life and academic life. I made new friend groups but I quickly learned that there are no number of friends that can substitute family. You need both, you need people. Honestly at this point, I'm beginning to contemplate different ways to commit suicide. I'm beginning to weigh the pros and cons of life and death, developing drug habits, and destroying healthy sleeping habits stressing over it all. Oh yeah, and I had to make sure I didn't fail out of school, and I was on Louisiana Tech's powerlifting team so I was doing all of this while maintaining a body weight of 130lbs or less and aiming to gain strength. Many things to balance at once but I wrote this because

I was also in Louisiana Tech's Poetry Society so this was written to be shared with them. I am very thankful for the Poetry Society because they did allow me to always have a release once a week. All part of the process for me to become the person, writing this book now. All for you to see into some of my darkest moments to help you through yours.

Crème de la Crème

Pardon my French, but you...
you was supposed to be the crème de la crème,
(1.5x-0.5x)
but I was so blinded by your glow I never pondered from where problems could stem.
I was too focused on giving you the world like in the movies,
I was thinkin dinners like wine and dine with ratatouille.
Thinkin Paris while Fall was in the air
but compared to your scent no perfume could even compare.
But maybe you not a French lover, maybe you prefer Spanish,
but my love has no boundaries so I'll speak until you understand it.
Mi amor no tiene fronteras,
I thought if I uttered these words Cupid would rush near us.
Allowing you to see that I wanted to be your matador,
to take on your bull and watch you do the flamenco some more.
But maybe you don't like Spanish so I'll say it in Italian,

il mio amore no ha confini, just tell me what language you wish I'd say it in and I'd make myself a genie.
Cause I see these other females tryna copy your foundation,
but I know where this style started, I won't follow imitation.
But the best part, is your head less gassed,
you the gelato to they ice cream,
you not even in the same class.
But this probably flying overhead cause you a Nubian queen,
You probably hear my passion but don't understand what I mean.
You probably prefer to see what I'm sayin,
hieroglyphics appears the easiest to understand.
The point is...I want to give you the world literally and physically,
just because of what your presence does for me mentally.
So could you POSSIBLY understand,
how bad it hurt when you said we'd be better as friends?

Poet's Words: Rejection is still strong, so at this point I think the list is too long to keep track of it all. From the body weight, the amount of alcohol consumption, lack of sleep, love life rejections, academics, and the list goes on. At this point, I was using concepts and different languages to express myself because I no longer felt as though my native tongue could even express how beat down and tired I was. It was in my highest level of discomfort that I actually learned a new language to express the way I felt. I viewed it like buying new paint brushes to paint with, or trying a new medium to display art on. This piece, I performed at an open mic at Grambling University and I will say Grambling is an experience when it comes to the arts. So with this piece, I learned a new way to express my heartbreak, and gained a core life memory that I'll have forever. In the words of Charles Dickens, "it was the best of times, it was the worst of times." Enjoy being uncomfortable from time to time, because you may wish you had later.

Chess games

I remember thinkin you were my queen,
I remember hearing things about you but I never let it intervene,
the way I felt about you,
to this day I still remember that smell about you.
But you saw me as just another pawn,
scheming to steal my heart from dusk to dawn.
I guess it was all just a game in my chest,
Wait...queen? Pawn? This was a chess game
but I was thinkin with my heart and not my brain.
How could I be so stupid?
How could I not see that this had nothing to do with Cupid?
I mean you even played me like a rook,
we only went out at night, that's the L I took.
You never called me your king and now I'm getting advice from a bishop,
but you won the game so you probably don't care to listen.
So now I defend myself so well I seem like a cold person,
but I have nothing left to defend yet I still feel something hurtin.

Poet's Words: Here I give away that...well...I like to play chess. I'm attracted to the game as every move matters and the possibilities seem endless. In this piece, for those who may be a bit confused, the knight is a chess piece that moves in the shape of an "L" but when I say I took an "L" I'm referring to taking a loss. Why was this piece important to helping your healing process? Want to know a secret? Most of the time when depression beats you down or your insecurities are beating on you, you either feel alone or spend most of your time alone. Learning chess and then wanting to get better at it made me seek more types of people I could connect with. It made me stop focusing so much on myself and start noticing the opportunities that were surrounding me. If you were to look around at your situation, what opportunities are you not noticing? Is there a person you think you may share similarities with that you haven't contacted in a while or maybe trying something new. I challenge you to go for a walk and when you see someone, talk to them as if you actually care about their life and have known them for years. You'd be surprised how healing it can be to get out of your own head from time to time. Connection with other people is what you were created to do, that's why it feels so good to be surrounded by people you care about. Oh yeah, and my bad streak of romantic rejection continues, but who's keeping count at this point?

Mental Exhaustion

Listen I ain't really felt like myself the last few weeks,
something just not right at the core like I'm tryna workout the obliques.
You see I keep pickin up this pen, tryna pin down what got me pinned down, (1.5x)
like where my friends now?
But I don't even wanna talk about it so I'm secluding myself, (1.5x)
looking in the mirror I start abusing myself. (1.5x)
Overdosing on insecurities, start reminiscing on the past so I see all my impurities. (1.5x)
But I'm so tired of fighting for optimism,
I'm trading sides, "Hey Arnold" is how I'm greeted by pessimism. (1.0x-0.5x)
I'm going Benedict cause I no longer see benefits (2x)
from allowing others to play ventriloquist (2x)
just to feel a pat on the back, (1.5x)
cause I feel without your hand my voice is taken back.
But you know what I'm not even worth voicing my opinions,
my whole life I'll probably never get to make my own decisions.
And nobody could ever understand what I'm feelin',
but when I pick up that .45 (four-five) and let it bust just know that I consented...

but I have to tell myself that all of this is just mental exhaustion,
and no need to lose myself twice if depression is what I'm lost in.

Poet's Words: Depression is real and I don't want to just say "depression is real and it affects many people all over the world everyday". No, I was there EVERY SINGLE DAY, wondering what the other side actually looks like because I didn't enjoy my reality and the constant pressure I felt. I had the negative self-talk where I would destroy myself for accomplishments that didn't meet someone else's standard for me. I've been tired of fighting, I've had suicide attempts that were obviously unsuccessful but the point is…EVERYTHING YOU ARE GOING THROUGH, is to help you get closer to the person you're supposed to be. Don't for a second allow yourself to think that the grass is greener on the other side, YOU ARE ENOUGH! As a matter of fact, you are more than enough and if you ever focus long enough to unlock your full potential, you'll see what I'm talking about but do not cheat the world out of your amazing creativity because you don't understand what you're turning into.

To Lead

Which way would you go if yo leader got lost?
If he found the way but losing himself was the cost?
Would you say its worth it and follow right behind
or would his sacrifice be in vain...like his mind?
As you can see my thoughts are getting heavy,
and I'm tryna be a leader but maybe I'm not ready.
(1.5x)
But this my ship and we not sinking yet so I'ma hold steady,
and if the ship have to sink then...well I'm ready.
Rather drown than hop ship,
and I still wonder whether my stubborn mind is a blessing or a gift.
Sometimes I just find myself wondering what if,
like what if I would just conform to perform the norm
and ignore the person I was born, (2x)
what if I had stayed at home without a loan to acquire wealth until I made my own, (2x)
what if I learn to use my gift, to move up like shift, (1.5x)
and let my pay be the people I lift, (1.5x)
what if I stop saying what if and made it happen,
would I go from quiet and humble to boastful and bragging? (0.5x)
What am I doing here? Tryna defy the odds that

mistakenly crept into my mind, nah open ya eyes and look at what you find.
An opportunity to be different
and somehow if you don't get all the things you envision
then you just another "I told you so" on which they'll be reminiscing.

Poet's Words: So even with me going through everything behind the scenes, can you believe people still looked to me as a leader? I'm in the mirror giving myself the negative self-talk of a lifetime and others are looking to me for guidance. Here's what I wish I could seen then that I can't unsee now…if people are looking up to you and you can't even look yourself in the eyes, why would they see so much potential in you? It's because no matter how hard you try, others can see the potential in you. No matter how far you go to destroy that potential, it will always resonate through you because it is who you are. You just haven't quite figured out how to be that person and it's ok. Just stay true to the process of figuring it out and when you're supposed to, you'll know exactly who you are and your potential.

Letter of a Wounded Soldier

To whomever comes next:

Every time I find a right hand, I hold her close to my heart, pledge my allegiance then she tear me apart. Scandal after scandal got us a lil' shaken up, so I find myself wondering who's not good enough. Cause I'd give her the world but I find it much too filthy, would give her my heart but it's much too empty. But I should've known she wouldn't tell me the ugly truth she was far too pretty, but beauty is only skin deep unlike the scars she'd give me. Cause I remember lookin into her eyes, when she told me them lies, so now I've tinted the window to my soul, I just bring up my pupils when she ask me about my goals. And I remember having cold feet and still placing my best foot forward, thinkin that she'd meet me halfway if I just kept walking towards her. But long story short, I cut off my right hand, so I can only give what I got left. I hope you understand.

Honestly,

The Injured

Poet's Words: In case you haven't peaked ahead, we're almost to college graduation and as you can see the mood, still hasn't exactly brightened up, but that's life. I could've camouflaged the pain of all those years and only put the "pretty" and "comforting" poems in this book but that wouldn't have been realistic. The hard truth is that sometimes dark times last longer than expected or intended. This just means that you have a few more realizations that have to be had before you can get to where you want to go. That's OK. Trust me, if you want a fulfilling life the goal is to have a marathon and not a sprint. You want to look back in your golden years and have memories, not reach the mountain top early with no one to tell about it. There is beauty even in the dark moments, if you're willing to look. Half the fun of life is connection with people, which is why it's more exciting to tell exciting stories of perseverance than to live a lonely, easy life of comfort.

Natural Beauty

Her beauty so natural, not knowing if her skin glows or if she's just that radiant,
I don't know if that's perfume, lotion or her natural fragrance.
She has me spacing out when I see the stars in her eyes,
now I just need to find where her love lies.
When she walks she's fluent like a calm stream,
and it turns on my Earth, Wind and Fire, call it a wet dream.
She controls all the elements, and avatar she seems,
but will she vanish from my world in this frozen scene?
How do I approach, direct or something more casual?
I don't know but it's like my legs were on automatic but my lips on manual.
At a loss for words I could only stare,
until her smile blinded me with a glare.
So naturally beautiful like the world following creation,
but I would've been nothing more than her mankind, an infestation.

Poet's Words: Wanna go back and read some of the stuff from high school? This is much better quality huh? The process, trust the process and enjoy the process.

Whatever is meant for you, you can't mess up. This piece, you can obviously see my confidence deteriorating but just because I see myself as a lower form of being doesn't mean that I can't recognize beauty. This is often the case with people who practice a lot of negative self-talk. So, if you have a friend that's always telling you how great you are, make sure to check on their mental health, make sure they're saying nice things about themselves as well. Feel free to start talking to yourself more positively too. Why does everyone else get kind words from you except for you?

Disconnected Pain

Four of my people have been taken,
I'm talkin bout by drugs don't be mistaken.
You can't do drugs cause DRUGS DO YOU
cause just one always turns into only two.
Then you gamble with life like double or nothin
and you already fell but lie, sayin you standing for something.
Can't even look yourself in the mirror, you like Forest you just keep runnin...
And that urge for more just keep comin,
and you sayin "well I'm just playin the cards I'm dealt",
but you playin solitaire so when you gone realize you playin yo' self.
And you say I'M just not livin to MY full potential,
well maybe not but at least I'm livin!! or was that supposed to be confidential? And you say I only talk this reckless behind my poetry,
but in reality I speak it this way so you'll end up quoting me.
So you remember some stuff you already know
and so those habits won't be the only thing that grow.
Cause you'll say you gotta do better just to hear me give advice.

Then go do it all over again without ever thinking twice.
And you wonder why I shake my head and have nothing more to say,
well would you if you saw somebody you love slippin away?
Yeah it just hit home didn't it!!
now you bouta lie again and say you done hittin it...
Please tell that lie to somebody else
and just continue to put your loved ones aside on the shelf.
Just allow us to see you suffer a pain we can't take away.
Cause you chose that over us,...so that's why we always look away.

Poet's Words: Love is funny huh? There so many different types, you know? Tough love, puppy love, fake love, honest love, but it hurts when you want more for someone you love and they don't. It does make it harder on you but you have to understand, you can only control one person...YOU. So love whoever it is, that you want more for, because they can't control you loving them. Just know the same way, they can't control you loving them through it all, you can't control they're decision making no matter how bad it hurts you. So protect yourself and your mental health but understand not everybody needs or even deserves the same type of love. And with that let's get to the pieces I wrote after graduation.

Post Graduation

Court Date

On my court date I'll be guilty of loyalty, probably have to pay royalties,
to some lady who cries "your honor, he's the one spoiling me!!"
So now we're to the point where she's leaving, after deceiving, (1.5x)
then had the nerve to file a grievance. (1.5x)
Got me evaluating the situation like what was I thinkin, (2x)
buying jewels for someone who was jaded, (2x)
throwing stones at a rocky situation, (2x)
bubble baths and foot rubs had her running outta patience, (2x)
breakfast in bed leading to debates as conversations. (1.5x)
Losing my peace tryna piece back everything falling apart, (1.5x)
she said I don't show my love as I stood in front of her pouring out my heart, (1x-0.5x)
till it went numb crazy how I felt dumb, labeling myself as a simpleton, (0.5x-1.0x)
so your honor this case is a simple one. (0.5x)
I'm the villain, not the victim, so send me to my pen where I can do some healing. Cause I don't feel better until I see it is written

and every punch feeling like my prescription.
But I refuse to pay a queen royalties,
when I walked her through life moments that soil tees,
and for all that I'm here calculating for court dates
and lawyer fees,
your honor please!!
I plead guilty of loyalty, cause any other way wouldn't sit right with me morally but whatever your decision, I'll take it on the chin accordingly.

Poet's Words: Listen, we're almost to the end and the worst part about getting closer to the destination is that the journey is almost over. That means that it gets drastically more uncomfortable right before it becomes freeing. In this piece, I express how I had done everything I knew to do in order to please a person I loved but at the end of the day it still wasn't enough. It made me feel I wasn't enough. It was after writing this piece that I realized you'll never be good enough to someone who projects their self-worth onto you. As people, we are always aiming for more, so even if you obtain the original mark that person had for you, the expectations are then heightened and you will never get to cross that finish line. You are not responsible for someone else's success or validation, just as no one is responsible for yours. You must define what your moral principles are and what you value in life. Your values may cost you some people who you thought you were close to and some opportunities in life but one missed opportunity will never be the last opportunity. Long story short, value the things that can't be bought.

Love is a Gamble

She was 5'2 like a deck of cards, she a black queen, me a black king,
felt like we was born a spread apart.
We vibe well together like a spread of hearts,
and every time I see her I think about how to play my cards.
Hope she not playing games cause I always seem to have the biggest heart in this game of hearts,
building myself up like a house of cards, before falling apart.
Careful not to volunteer, myself for a situation like solitaire,
cause playin myself...that game ain't ever fair.
So I'm poker face no matter how much my heart keep beating,
and I'm holding my breath just so you don't hear me breathing,
it got you wondering what I'm thinking. Here's what I'm thinking,
can you play gin in the spotlight at the family reunion, (1.5x)
take hits during blackjack and still wake up for communion? (1.5x)
And I'm not sayin' show your hand cause of course that would be stupid,

but give me a cue, don't leave me sittin' here clueless.
And she answered me quick callin a spade a spade,
say she rather that than the club, her words
surpassing her age.
If she give me her heart I'll give her a diamond,
what a story this could be depending on the timing.
Could she be the one queen to suit me, deal me in
cause player beats house in this movie.

Poet's Words: What goes around comes around. Everything will happen for you exactly when it's supposed to. Genuine people meet genuine people, if not immediately, eventually. The question is will you remain generous long enough to receive the generosity you put out into the world? The healed version of you that is working in your purpose attracts to you the things you always wanted and needed.

Walking By Faith

How you been? Suicidal, why you think I'm in my Bible.
Questioning my sanity, my purpose in humanity,
I'm even questioning God, like "do you still have a plan for me??"
Feeling forgotten, like it was a human emotion,
got me spending time with God, call it daily devotions.
If I'm not forsaken, then are you breaking my heart so that it don't harden,
and Lord if I'm being disrespectful I beg your pardon.
I just don't understand, everyday I seek wisdom,
pray to you that my sins are forgiven,
but the desires of my heart are what never seems mentioned.
Father I don't get it, why do I keeping waking up,
I do everything I can, but never seems enough.
Am I even doing the things for which I was created,
or was I a creation you designed to be complacent.
I pray whatever my purpose you come place it,
on my heart, heal my heart and help me kill demons that I'm face with.
You said it is written so you gave me a pen and this pigment,
so I can see the destination without the confines of religion.

I feel your love amplified when the world treats me different,
so when I come to the crossroads, I take the path to keep living.

Poet's Words: I think this is the most important part of the healing process. Once you've learned yourself enough to search for your purpose, you'll notice many things go away. Like questioning your self-worth, getting bogged down in your own insecurities, instead you begin to notice that you are enough and you just want to do the thing you're really good at. Now for me specifically, I noticed this when I searched for God (yes I believe in God) because I knew I was capable of doing more than what I was doing so I began praying for awareness of what I was good at that would help others. Thus this book began after realizing I had already been writing for over a decade. Now I know you may not believe in God but I don't believe in coincidence and I think it's very coincidental that I write a poetry book I had no intentions of writing over a decade after I started writing poetry. All grand design in my opinion. I say all that to say everything you're going through you're strong enough to make it through. You'll have a few break downs along the way but that just makes it worth something to you when you accomplish what you were put here to do. If we believe in the same God, always remember you are never forgotten.

Classical Heartbreak

I stroked you like piano keys, together we made beautiful music,
till I only heard symphonies, all these instrumentals inconclusive,
lacking lyrics to confirm communication,
so I'm tuning out with our lack of conversation.
We don't fight, so tell me... what's this, a(bout)?
Screaming I don't hear you, but do you ever close your mouth?
Waiting for permission to broaden your perspective
cause if I raise my voice, you manipulate the perception,
your introspection, projecting...itself onto me
so good enough for you was impossible for me.
But that's ok, I'm willing to heal together,
let's not tip toe around how we can build together,
but then I noticed you always skipped that part that said 'till forever.
So now I have a scar that I'll feel forever.
But with time things heal, how much of that did we kill together?
Killing time, drinking wine,
till hours passed and your hourglass didn't seem so fine,
nothing to do with your diet but more with your mind,

cause you never entice my mind, never stopped to ask if I was fine,
you stole my heart, that's a crime,
but we can gel together if you'd be mine,...
years later no bond, just wasted time.
So I had to stop taking ownership of someone who isn't mine,
had to reconsider love and how it should be define,
still dealing with the pain, I guess its all by grand design.

Poet's Words: Welcome to the destination, the healed version. Not as beautiful as you thought it would be huh? So listen, initially the healed version of you is beautiful on the outside before it's beautiful within. Think of it as cleaning out your room at your parents' house. Initially it hurts because you have so many years of memories in that room so it hurts to have to take down all the pictures and clean out your closet. The room looks lifeless once you've moved all your things out, however when you move everything into your new place everything is so much better. It feels so freeing being able to hang your picture on the wall of your new place wherever you want or shower for as long as you choose. As more time passes it's so freeing that you never want to go back to your parents' house. With time you develop a new normal and you have all the lessons (your paraphernalia) that you had from before. The first few nights sleeping in a place of your own is new, but with time you will heal and be stronger than before.

Glass Ice Cube

It broke, it's broken, what more could happen?
It was glass now it's ice, cause there's no more passion.
We butted heads, you took my love and held it ransom,
but why you would do it, I never could fathom.
Can you imagine my reaction?
When I looked in the mirror watching the transformation happen?
I saw my eyes as they blackened, hunch back while my chest crackin,
tryna smile for the viewer like an awards show reaction.
'Till I hit the floor and everything blackened,
when I came to, it was true, I was free from enchantment,
so now I wish you no bad, cause what happened happened.
And I'm coo' on most of the females I'm attracting,
I mean no disrespect but I have no more time for distractions,
I've become so strategic I'm planning every action.
Cause I gotta keep my brother, my niece, see how things keep addin?
But now I'm alone I can't even ask madden.
So yes…it broke, it's broken, what more could happen?
I could never feel happy, but I can't stop laughing.

Poet's Words: How do you know when you've healed? When you can discuss the things you once never wanted to talk about. When you are comfortable with every decision that was a mistake, can be held accountable for the choices but understanding that it wasn't a version of you to be ashamed of. Broken people display harmful habits and usually make poor decisions. You are not the first person to fight through depression, suicidal thoughts, or insecurities. You will not be the last to fight with depression, suicidal thoughts, or insecurities. Do not allow your past to shame your present and don't spend the present wasting your future. You have every tool you need for you to get to where you need to go, just put one foot in front of the other and express yourself because we need it. The world, the people who you walk past and say nothing to everyday, we all need you to be your naturally creative self so that together we build a more beautiful tomorrow. Don't take your dreams to the grave, you won't see half your potential if you do. And you'll meet amazing people on the way, just…get comfortable in your skin. The answer isn't something outside of you, it's everything inside of you. You just have to bring it out.

www.ingramcontent.com/pod-product-compliance
Lightning Source LLC
Chambersburg PA
CBHW032214040426
42449CB00005B/596